The Good-Night Blessing Book

written and illustrated by
NANCY WILLARD

THE BLUE SKY PRESS
An Imprint of Scholastic Inc. · New York

THE BLUE SKY PRESS

For information regarding permission, please write to:
Permissions Department,
The Blue Sky Press, an imprint of Scholastic Inc.,
555 Broadway, New York, New York 10012.

The Blue Sky Press is a registered trademark of Scholastic Inc.

Library of Congress Cataloging-in-Publication Data

Willard, Nancy.

The good-night blessing book /
written and illustrated by Nancy Willard.

p.   cm.

ISBN 0-590-62393-1

1. Prayer–Juvenile poetry.   2. Children's poetry, American.   I. Title.

PS3573.I444G6   1996   811'.54-dc20   95-26167   CIP   AC

12 11 10 9 8 7 6 5 4 3 2 1   6 7 8 9/9 0 1/0

Printed in Singapore   46

First printing, September 1996

FOR GAIL KINN

Bless breakfast made

by milky light

when morning

blows away the night.

Bless cups and pitchers,

pots and spoons,

candles and keys,

the bride and groom.

Bless open windows,

doors that sing,

rooms that invite

the forest in.

Bless vegetables,

bless ferns and flowers,

cities with clocks

that free the hours.

Bless new-washed clothes,

the Milky Way,

and those we love

who do not stay

but journey out,

so fast, so far

they break bread with

the evening star.

Around my house

the dark runs deep,

so bless me

when I fall asleep.

ACKNOWLEDGMENTS

The background to the image on the title page is from the painting *The Open Missal* by Ludger tom Ring, the Younger, courtesy of the Frances Lehman Loeb Art Center, Vassar College, Poughkeepsie, New York. Used by permission.

Special thanks to Magic City Milk & Ice Company for the use of its milk bottle in this book. Magic City is a registered trademark of Magic City Milk & Ice Company. Additional special thanks to First National Stores Incorporated for the use of its trademark, Finast. Finast is a registered trademark of First National Stores Incorporated.

The background to the images for "Bless breakfast made by milky light . . ." is by Stephen Mackey, courtesy of Lip International, Manchester, England. Used by permission.

The key holder used within the image for ". . . candles and keys . . ." was created by Joanne Burlingame. Used by permission.

The photograph within the image for ". . . and those we love . . ." is of Jerome Badanes, novelist and scriptwriter for the film, *Image Before My Eyes*, and was taken by Eric Lindbloom.

The figure within the image for ". . . so bless me . . ." is by Marcia Wilson. Copyright © Marcia Sandmeyer Wilson. Used by permission.

The background to the image for ". . . so bless me . . ." is by Renee Graef. Copyright © Renee Graef. Used by permission.

The figure on the back cover is by Karen Germany, courtesy of Brent Germany and Karen Germany, K V K, Incorporated. Used by permission.

.

The photographs in this book were taken by Nancy Willard.
The text type was set in Canterbury Old Style Bold by WLCR New York, Inc.
Color separations were made by Bright Arts, Ltd., Singapore.
Printed and bound by Tien Wah Press, Singapore
Production supervision by Angela Biola
Designed by Kathleen Westray